Sandy Koufax

Geraldine Giordano

the rosen publishing group's
rosen central

To my brother, Tony, and my uncles, Anthony and
Reno, the biggest baseball fans I know.
And to little Franco—a future fanatic!

Published in 2003 by The Rosen Publishing Group, Inc.
29 East 21st Street, New York, NY 10010

First Edition

Library of Congress Cataloging-in-Publication Data

Giordano, Geraldine.
Sandy Koufax / by Geri Giordano.
   p. cm. — (Baseball Hall of Famers)
Summary: Profiles the youngest man inducted into the
Baseball Hall of Fame who, while playing for his hometown
team, the Brooklyn Dodgers, began as wild and uncoordinated but became one of the best pitchers of all time.
Includes bibliographical references and index.
ISBN 0-8239-3603-1 (lib. bdg.)
1. Koufax, Sandy, 1935– —Juvenile literature. 2. Baseball
players—United States—Biography—Juvenile literature.
[1. Koufax, Sandy, 1935– 2. Baseball players.]
I. Title. II. Series.
GV865.K67 G56 2002
796.357'092—dc21

                                          2002000279

Manufactured in the United States of America

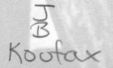

Contents

Introduction 5

1 A Brooklyn Kid Makes It Big 9

2 A Star Pitcher Is Born! 35

3 The Perfect Game 64

4 Sandy Koufax Retires 77

5 The Baseball Hall of Fame 91

Glossary 102

For More Information 104

For Further Reading 106

Bibliography 107

Index 109

Sandy Koufax was one of the best baseball pitchers ever. He threw a National League–record four no-hitters, including a perfect game. Twice he struck out 18 batters in a game, and in 1965 he got 382 strikeouts, a major-league record at the time.

Introduction

Sandy Koufax is considered one of the best pitchers in baseball history. He threw the ball fast and hard. Batters often struck out against him. Studying his moves and pitches made no difference. Koufax could beat the best batter at the plate!

Koufax received many honors throughout his baseball career. Three Cy Young Awards proved he had incredible skill. Becoming the youngest member of the Baseball Hall of Fame only reinforced what fans, sportswriters, and his colleagues thought of him—Sandy Koufax played the game of baseball with excellence, elegance, and dead-on pitching.

But he didn't start out that way. Like many athletes, Koufax had to work hard. For years he battled to control the ball. He attributed this struggle to two things. He played in the majors

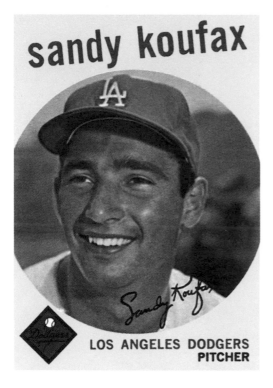

sandy koufax

LOS ANGELES DODGERS
PITCHER

"Hitting against Sandy Koufax is like eating soup with a fork!" Pittsburgh Pirates batter Willie Stargell said of Koufax. Despite his short career, Koufax left a lasting impression on the game, and his baseball cards are still treasured today.

before he was ready, so he hadn't had enough time to perfect his skills. And he sometimes had mental blocks when standing on the pitcher's mound.

Later in his career, Sandy Koufax had to overcome public scrutiny because of his religious beliefs. Koufax came from a traditional Jewish family. He refused to pitch on High Holy Days, even if they fell during a World Series. Many people felt he chose his religion over his career. Sandy Koufax chose to do what he knew was right.

Koufax developed into an incredibly accomplished baseball player. On September 9, 1965, Koufax became the eighth pitcher in the history of baseball to pitch a perfect game. What made this feat especially amazing was that Koufax had been battling an elbow injury during the entire 1965 baseball season.

On November 1, 1966, Sandy Koufax received his third Cy Young Award. He was the first pitcher to receive the Cy Young that many times. The list of his accomplishments is long. This is the story of Sandy Koufax and his life as one of baseball's most beloved pitchers.

Koufax won three Cy Young Awards at a time when the award went to the best pitcher in all of major league baseball, not just in the American League or in the National League. Many believe that if it hadn't been for injuries, Koufax would have won more.

A Brooklyn Kid Makes It Big

Sanford "Sandy" Braun was born on December 30, 1935, in Brooklyn, New York. His parents, Evelyn and Jack Braun, divorced when Sandy was three. His father didn't spend much time with Sandy after the divorce. When Jack Braun remarried six years later, all contact with his son ceased. Evelyn was an accountant who supported Sandy by herself until she met and married Irving Koufax, a Manhattan lawyer.

Irving and Sandy became very close, and Sandy adopted his stepfather's last name. Sandy also gained a sister, Edith, who was Irving's daughter from a previous marriage. When asked today, Sandy says that Irving Koufax was the only father he ever knew.

Irving Koufax played an important role in Sandy's life. He taught both of his children many things, including the importance of strong

Sandy Koufax's biological father, Jack Braun, took these pictures of Sandy at batting practice when he was eight years old.

morals and values. He took them to shows at the Yiddish theater in New York City, which was both a bonding and cultural experience for the family. Irving also encouraged Sandy to pursue sports, particularly basketball and baseball.

As a child, Sandy loved basketball. He played in the summertime with his friends. Whether it was in the schoolyard, on the playground, or at the Jewish community center,

Sandy played constantly. If there weren't enough players for complete teams, Sandy would play three-man basketball with the kids he could find. On days when kids weren't around, he was content to shoot baskets on his own.

When Sandy was eleven, his family moved to Long Island, New York. He didn't have many chances to play sports while he lived there because there weren't many playing fields or basketball courts. After four years, his family moved back to Brooklyn.

The Ice Cream League

A neighborhood man named Secol, nicknamed "Pop" by the kids, decided to create a baseball league. It was dubbed the Ice Cream League, and the kids played on the Parade Grounds in Flushing, Queens. The Parade Grounds consisted of ten baseball diamonds and a playground. It was every kid's dream. The league, made up of kids ages fourteen and older, had lots of teams. Sandy was the pitcher for the Tomahawks. By sixteen, he already had a reputation for being a wild pitcher. It seemed as if he could either walk a batter or strike him out. There was never any middle ground. Despite his lack of control, Sandy's strength and his ability to throw fast pitches began to show.

Senior Year—a Basketball Star?

When Sandy was still a student at Lafayette High School in Brooklyn, he was on the basketball team. In fact, Sandy was the team's star forward. In his senior year, he was named All-City forward by the Schoolboy Basketball Writers of the Metropolitan District. After Sandy won this honor, college scouts began to take notice of his talent. Offers poured in from top basketball schools around the country!

University of Cincinnati

Sandy Koufax wanted to become an architect. The University of Cincinnati had one of the leading schools in architecture at the time. This was the deciding factor for Sandy. He accepted a basketball scholarship and attended the University of Cincinnati in the fall of 1953.

Koufax, pictured here in his University of Cincinnati baseball uniform, attended the school on a basketball scholarship. But his baseball skills soon eclipsed his basketball abilities and many major league baseball teams were offering him contracts. He left school to go to the majors.

Averaging 9.7 points per game, he was considered a star athlete. But becoming an athlete was the farthest thing from Sandy's mind! He was a quiet guy. Being in the spotlight wasn't important to him.

The varsity basketball coach was also the University of Cincinnati's baseball coach. Once the basketball season had ended, Sandy asked to try out for the baseball team. His friends were on the team and he wanted to join them. He knew he wasn't a very good hitter, but he told the coach that he could pitch.

During his freshman baseball season, Sandy won three games and lost one. He struck out 51 batters in 32 innings, and walked 30 batters. Once again, he caught the attention of scouts. This time, they noticed his baseball skills.

Summer Camp and His Big Break

In the summer of 1954, Sandy Koufax was a counselor at Camp Chi-Wan-Da in Kingston, New York. He already had a reputation for being a great athlete. The kids at the camp loved to watch him play. Rumors flew around camp that baseball scouts were trying to sign him. The rumors proved to be true when scouts from teams around the country arrived to watch him play.

Sandy was invited to try out for many different teams. When Sandy tried out for the New York Giants, he played horribly, hitting the screen behind the catcher. He is reported to have said that he pitched so poorly because he had been so nervous.

When the Brooklyn Dodgers offered him a contract, he took time to consider it because the Pittsburgh Pirates were also trying to sign him. Because he was in demand, Sandy requested a bonus payment in addition to a salary. He asked for this extra money because if he left the university to play baseball, he would lose his scholarship. He could use the extra money to return to school once the baseball season ended.

That summer, after camp, Sandy Koufax signed a contract to play for his hometown team, the Brooklyn Dodgers, in New York City.

Koufax's pitching at the University of Cincinnati caught the attention of major league baseball scouts. Having signed with the Dodgers, Koufax is flanked by Dodgers' scout Alex Campanis *(left)* and Dodgers' vice president Fresco Thompson.

Bonus Baby

Sandy Koufax was considered a "bonus baby" because his contract included an extra $14,000, a lot of money in the 1950s. At the time, baseball rules stated that he was required to stay on the Brooklyn Dodgers' roster for two years. Sandy's bonus cemented the agreement. Unfortunately, the agreement prevented him from pitching in the minor leagues, where he could get important practice and experience.

First, he was required to attend spring training at the Dodgers' camp in Vero Beach, Florida. A baseball training camp is where all team players gather before the beginning of a season. They practice, develop good eating habits, and get medical exams. Coaches pay attention to the performance of each player and decide who will make the playing roster for that year. This is especially important for a rookie because he is a first-year player. Scouting reports inform coaches about how a new player had performed in the past. Spring training allows the coach to see this player in action for the first time.

Koufax received a uniform and all the necessary equipment. There were many rules at spring training that players had to follow:

- No overeating while in training.
- No smoking in the cafeteria.
- No drinking or gambling.
- No snacking between meals.
- No baseball shoes in the buildings.
- Players must return before curfew.
- Players must not go out after curfew.

This 1956 picture shows Sandy Koufax *(second from top, right)* stretching with Dodgers' teammates during spring training. The Dodgers won the League pennants in 1955 and 1956, but Koufax's contribution was marginal, as he pitched only 100 ⅓ innings.

Koufax must have felt a little overwhelmed when he walked into the clubhouse that first morning and saw so many great ballplayers. Pee Wee Reese, Roy Campanella, Joe Black, and Jackie Robinson were there. Many rookies have said that they were awed when they met their famous teammates. They still viewed them as idols and had a hard time thinking of them as peers, as members of the same team.

Dodger manager Walter Alston gave the rookies a pep talk, telling them to ask questions of the older players, who were there to help. Alston wanted his players to treat each other equally.

When Koufax got on the pitcher's mound at training camp, he was uncoordinated. Players watched him throw pitches over the heads of catchers. To prevent sports reporters from catching a glimpse of Koufax's wild pitching, he was sent to the "string area" of the camp. Pitchers with difficulties were sent there to practice privately. It was a remote field where spectators and the media were less likely to spot wild playing and report on it.

Koufax *(center)* cracks a smile with Dodgers' manager Walter Alston *(right)* and Dodgers' right-handed pitcher Don Drysdale.

Dodgers' pitching coach Joe Becker taught Koufax to relax and concentrate. He suggested that Koufax take his time when he pitched. Because Koufax was so nervous, he had a tendency to throw pitches one after another, with little break time between them. His muscles began to get sore. Becker told Koufax that if he started to hurt, he had to take a break. Learning to pace himself between pitches would be key. The Dodgers did not want an injured rookie pitcher.

During his downtime at the camp, Koufax spent a lot of time reading. When he left the compound, he loved to visit downtown Vero Beach, where he enjoyed studying the architecture of the homes and office buildings. At that time, ranch and split-level homes were the latest style. Koufax still dreamed of becoming an architect.

When people asked him about his baseball career, he thoughtfully answered that he figured he wouldn't be put into too many games during his first two years. He imagined that he'd be benched a lot during the season. He expected to learn from watching the experienced pitchers.

Koufax decided that he'd give five years to baseball. He assumed that the last three years he would spend on a Dodgers' minor league team. Once he completed five years, he'd go back to college to get his degree in architecture.

The Rookie Plays Ball

Koufax was put on the disabled list for the first months of his first professional season. Finally, his manager felt he was ready to play. On June 6, 1955, Koufax pitched two innings of a game the Dodgers were losing to the Milwaukee Braves. Koufax allowed one hit, walked one batter, and struck out two others. On July 6, he got his first major-league start against the Pittsburgh Pirates. In five innings, he threw 106 pitches, which was normal for a full, nine-inning game.

A month later Koufax was given the chance to start another game. On August 27, he pitched against Cincinnati. This game turned out to be special. Koufax pitched a two-hit shutout, and the Dodgers won 1–0.

Koufax broke a National League pitching record that day, striking out 14 players! His teammates rushed to the pitcher's mound to congratulate their rookie. Baseball commentators were impressed. They reported that he had thrown some of the fastest pitches they had ever seen. Batters had watched the ball shoot past them.

Koufax poses with the ball used when he pitched a record 14 strikeouts in a game against Cincinnati in 1955. The game, which was his first major league victory, was a near shutout, as he held Cincinnati to only two hits.

Koufax was focused and confident on the mound, a deadly combination for any batter. Word got back to Brooklyn that Koufax was going to be the next baseball star.

The Dodgers made it to the 1955 World Series that postseason and they won. Koufax received his first World Series ring even though he hadn't pitched in any of the games!

When he returned home, Koufax took courses at Columbia University in New York City. He planned to attend school for one semester each winter so that he could complete his architecture degree in four years.

Koufax returned to the Dodgers for the 1956 baseball season with more confidence. He had survived his rookie year and was looking forward to getting more pitching time.

Unfortunately, the opposing teams were able to get the best of him during the first couple of games. By season's end, Koufax had pitched in only 16 games and had started just 10 of them. That totaled 59 innings. His record was two wins and four losses with an ERA (earned run average) of 4.88—not great for a pitcher.

His teammates teased him about his wild throws, but they respected his fastball. Sportswriters and commentators said that Koufax had natural technique because his pitching motions could not be taught. They were impressed by the way he was able to change the movement of the ball. His ball moved once it was halfway to the plate. Sometimes it would drop lower. Sometimes it would sail a little higher. But he still had to work on his control.

The Dodgers found themselves in the World Series in 1956, this time against the Yankees. They lost in seven games. Koufax, who did not participate in postseason play, watched from the bench.

Bonus Baby No More

Once the first month of the 1957 baseball season passed, Koufax's two-year obligation with the Dodgers was complete. The team was free to send him to one of its minor league farms where he could get in more pitching time and gain more experience. Koufax had become used to living like a major leaguer, and he was anxious about where he'd end up. He knew that minor leaguers spent most nights traveling to away games, sleeping in uncomfortable buses, and grabbing quick bites at local burger joints.

On May 16, Alston announced that Koufax would be the starting pitcher in a game against the Chicago Cubs. Koufax was thrilled—he pitched a great game. He struck out thirteen batters, bringing his total to 35 in only 27 innings of the new season! After that incredible performance, Koufax had earned his pitching spot in the Dodgers' rotation.

He experienced ups and downs throughout the 1957 season. Dodgers' officials thought about sending him down to one of their farm teams in the minor leagues, but they were torn. Koufax threw with incredible speed, but his wild pitches made him dangerous to batters and catchers.

By season's end, he had started 13 games of the 34 he pitched. His ERA had jumped up a little, to 3.89. He had won five games and lost four.

Center fielder Duke Snider *(center)* picks chocolate from a giant candy banner at a banquet for the Dodgers, who moved from Brooklyn to Los Angeles in 1958. Known as the Silver Fox and the Duke of Flatbush, Snider is the only player to hit four homers in two different World Series. He was inducted into the Hall of Fame in 1980.

Moving to California

In 1958, the Brooklyn Dodgers moved to California and became the Los Angeles Dodgers. Like the other players, Koufax missed New York City. He longed for the old stadium, the passionate fans who either loved them or hated them, the old broadcasters, and even the organist, who played "Happy Birthday" to the players.

Even so, this was Koufax's most productive season so far. He won 11 games and lost 11 games. He improved his strikeout record, beating 131 batters. But he also walked 105 batters.

In the 1959 season, Koufax came close to something incredible. It was in June, during a game against Philadelphia. Koufax had struck out 16 batters in eight innings. If he could get one more batter out, he'd tie Dizzy Dean's National League record of 17. If he could strike out two more batters, he'd tie Bob Feller's American League record. The anticipation mounted, but Koufax was not able to beat either record. As Phillies' manager Gene Mauch said, Koufax was the only pitcher who could tease batters with his fastball. His taunting dared the batters to try to hit. Although Koufax didn't break records that day, he won the game, raising his season stats to six wins and two losses.

But Koufax was not to be underestimated, as he proved two months later on August 31, 1959. The game was in Los Angeles against the San Francisco Giants, in front of 82,974 fans. Koufax was throwing heat, and had eliminated

Koufax shares a smile with Dodgers' teammate, outfielder Wally Moon, after they played in a dramatic game against the San Francisco Giants in 1959. Koufax struck out a record 18 players in nine innings to set a new National League record. Moon hit a three-run homer in the ninth inning, driving in Koufax to clinch the game 5–2.

fifteen batters by the eighth inning. The score was tied 2–2, going into the ninth inning. At the top of the ninth, Koufax struck out three batters in row! Not only did he break Dizzy Dean's National League record, making it his own, he also tied Bob Feller's record of 18 strikeouts.

The Dodgers were up in the bottom of the ninth. The first batter struck out. Next came Koufax. Since he was known to be a poor batter, the Giants figured they'd get an easy out with him at the plate. But they were wrong. Koufax hit a single! The next batter, Junior Gilliam, got another single, and Wally Moon hit a home run. The Dodgers won, 5–2!

Koufax's strikeout frenzy continued. By September 1959, just a month later, he had thrown 38 strikeouts in three consecutive games. Sandy Koufax, surpassing Bob Feller and Walter Johnson, broke yet another major league record.

The Dodgers went on to beat Milwaukee and win the 1959 pennant. They made it to the World Series, to play against the Chicago White Sox. Koufax was called to pitch, his first time ever during a World Series game.

Although the Dodgers lost Game 1, Koufax did a good job on the mound. He spent Games 2 and 3 in the bullpen, watching his fellow pitchers win the games. With the series at 2–1 in favor of his team, Alston decided to start Koufax in Game 4. Unfortunately, Koufax pitched wildly, giving up a grand slam. The Dodgers lost the game 1–0.

The Dodgers managed to win the next two games, and the World Series, with the help of Johnny Podres, who won Game 6 for them. Koufax watched from the bench.

Norm Sherry

In 1960, Koufax showed noticeable differences in his pitching. He was throwing fewer pitches and getting more strikes. He was thinking about where he wanted the ball to be when it crossed the plate. Oddly, it was the first year that he had more losses than wins. His record was eight wins and 13 losses. But this didn't seem to bother Alston because he saw Koufax's improvements.

People have reported that this change came about for Koufax as a result of a discussion he had with Dodgers' backup catcher Norm Sherry. The two men, who were roommates during spring training that year, had a casual conversation on a bus ride to an exhibition game. Sherry suggested that Koufax concentrate more on throwing the ball over the plate rather than throwing for speed. He said that Koufax should think about varying his pitches. Sherry must have gotten

Right-handed pitcher Don Drysdale proved to be a reliable asset for the Los Angeles Dodgers at a time when southpaw Koufax still had control problems.

through to him. Koufax began throwing with rhythm. He concentrated on perfecting his curveball. He introduced change-ups to the batters.

Don Drysdale had also been a rookie pitcher for the Dodgers with Koufax. He was a big right-handed pitcher who received a bonus but had been farmed out to the minors. By 1957, he was back with the Dodgers. That season he won 17 games and lost nine.

Drysdale's 2.66 ERA tied the National League second-place record that year. This was an incredible feat for such a young pitcher, and it had earned him a spot in the rotation of Dodgers pitchers.

Koufax wanted to begin pitching more often now that he had found his control. He was six seasons into his baseball career. He had become a confident pitcher with incredible speed and power. He asked to be put in more games because he felt that getting too much rest and playing infrequently was contributing to his poor control.

1961

Koufax felt most comfortable during the 1961 season. He found the plate and began to enjoy himself. He won 18 games and lost 13. His 3.52 ERA was better than some of his fellow teammates'. He even set a new National League record of 269 strikeouts. His walks dropped to 96. By June, he had delivered his fifth consecutive complete game victory.

Koufax's pitching coach, Joe Becker, attributed Koufax's success to changes in his movements. Koufax was shortening his stride. Instructed to throw curveballs when he was behind in the count, he was learning strategy. Batters who expected him to pitch a fastball straight down the middle were caught off-guard.

Alston, pleased with Koufax's performance, admitted that more playing time was highly beneficial. In the past, the team had had many pitchers. Koufax had to earn his right to be in the pitching rotation.

Koufax still agrees with what Becker and Alston have said about his pitching. But Koufax has his own opinions. He feels that, as a young player, he would have benefited from having played in the minors. With more playing time, he would have practiced and learned more. Instead of reaching his baseball goals in three years, it took six.

A Star Pitcher Is Born!

Koufax was the master of two pitches, the fastball and the curveball. He had an advantage over most other pitchers because he had long, slender fingers that he could easily wrap around the ball. He could snap the ball out of his hand as he threw it. This gave the ball an unusual kind of momentum and spin. Batters could see exactly what kind of pitch Koufax was going to throw because he kept his hands close to his head. But this didn't matter. They watched the ball fly across the plate and heard a loud "Strike!" from the umpire.

On June 30, 1962, about halfway through the season, Koufax proved he could undo just about any batter with his pitching. The Dodgers were playing against the New York Mets. The score was 4–0. The Dodgers were in the lead in the bottom of the first inning.

During the second inning, there were some close calls. Frank Thomas of the Mets would have gotten a base hit, but shortstop Maury Wills made a great play. Richie Ashburn attempted a hit in the sixth inning, only to have Tommy Davis grab it to save his team. Ashburn again, in the ninth inning, tried to foil Koufax's plans by hitting the ball long to left field, out of Davis's reach. Fortunately for Koufax, the ball went foul.

The only men to get on base that night walked. Sandy Koufax had pitched a no-hitter! The crowd of more than 30,000 fans went wild. Koufax's teammates went wild! Koufax went wild! He had struck out every New York Mets player at least once!

This added another 13 strikeouts to his already incredible record. As of June, he had 183 strikeouts in 150 innings under his belt for the 1962 season.

In the clubhouse, players celebrated Sandy's achievement and their win. One by one they congratulated him. They joked with him and hung up signs to kid him. One sign said, "June 30, 1962, Sandy Koufax's Perfect Game. 0 for 4.

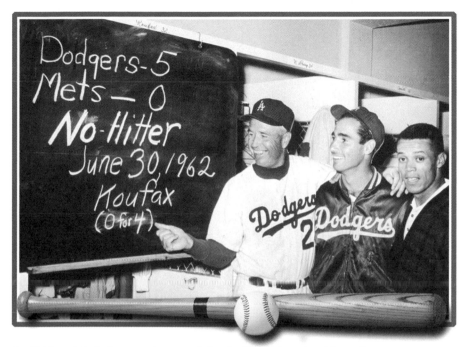

By 1962, with help from pitching coach Joe Becker and catcher Norm Sherry, Koufax was pitching more accurately and effectively. He threw the first of his four no-hitters against the New York Mets in 1962.

Some No-hitter!" They were referring to the fact that Sandy had not gotten a hit while at bat.

The media asked Koufax if he had used any strategy to win this game. Koufax, always a modest and professional ballplayer, said he believed that luck played a huge part in his success. He earned a raise as a result of the game. Companies wanted him to sponsor their products. He had made it. Sandy Koufax was a baseball superstar!

Sandy Koufax throws the final pitch of his no-hitter against the New York Mets on June 30, 1962. The Dodgers won the game 5–0.

The Pain Begins

By July 1962, Koufax developed a severe pain in his left palm and middle finger. He had been straining to grip the ball. Until then, he had been quiet about the pain. But he was finding it harder and harder to throw his curveball.

By the All-Star Game that year, Koufax's middle finger was becoming numb. Since it hurt him to pitch his curveball, he began to favor his fastball. Soon his finger developed a blister, got swollen, and became discolored. Koufax wondered about how this could have happened. His doctors told him that it had to do with his circulation. They wanted him to rest. But this was the last thing that Koufax wanted!

He felt that his team needed him on the mound. So between innings, he applied an electric heating pad to his hand. When a Dodgers' trainer, Wayne Anderson, revealed that Koufax was experiencing shooting pain in his arm, everyone on the team was concerned. Koufax was worried, too.

Koufax was sent back to Los Angeles, where doctors looked at his hand. IIe was diagnosed with Reynaud's phenomenon. This is a circulatory problem that begins with a blood clot. In Koufax's case, the blood clot was in his palm. The clot reduces the amount of blood that can reach a finger. The finger becomes sensitive at first, and then it becomes completely numb. This disease is predominant in adult men in their twenties. The doctors thought that this may have happened as a result of the extreme force and grip Koufax used to pitch his fastballs.

The doctors also told Koufax that he was in danger of losing his finger completely! They prescribed four different drugs to help it heal.

Koufax feared that he wouldn't be able to pitch the same way. He was also afraid that the condition would return.

When he was asked why he had waited so long to have his finger checked, Koufax explained why he was hesitant. He felt that the team needed him because his teammate, Johnny Podres, was having a bad season.

This composite of photos shows Sandy Koufax's pitching action. One of the fastest pitchers ever, Koufax initially had control trouble. Once he overcame that, he was nearly unbeatable. In fact, after an injury in 1963, he pitched 11 shutout games.

Koufax spent a lot of time running in the outfield while his finger healed. He couldn't pitch the ball to his teammates and he couldn't catch grounders during practice. It didn't look like Koufax would be pitching for the remainder of the season. Disappointed, his manager thought it was best to wait it out.

By September, Koufax asked for a chance to play. He pitched fastballs during practice. After a few minutes, he said that his finger didn't hurt. This was encouraging. After more practice, Koufax convinced both Alston and Becker that he was ready to get back on the mound. It had taken nine weeks for his finger to heal.

Back in the Game

On September 27, 1962, Koufax played his first game back from the injury against the San Francisco Giants. But he still wasn't playing his best. Reliever Ron Perranoski took over after a few innings, and the Dodgers lost the game 8–2.

The Dodgers continued on to the play-offs. Koufax played once, but he still wasn't in top form. Felipe Alou doubled, and Willie Mays hit a home run during the first inning. When Jim Davenport hit a home run in the second inning, Koufax was replaced. The Dodgers lost the game, 8–0. They lost the play-offs, too.

That winter, during the off-season, Koufax appeared on Milton Berle's television show with a bunch of his teammates: Maury Wills, Frank Howard, Don Drysdale, Willie Davis, and Duke Snider. Dressed in black tuxedos, top hats, and silver-topped canes, they performed a song and dance routine. During the show, Milton Berle asked Koufax about his finger. Koufax said it was better and ready to perform.

The 1963 Season

The Dodgers had a good season in 1963, making it to the championships. Koufax looked like he was back in form, winning 14 games into July.

One of those winning games was another no-hitter, this time against the Giants. The game was on a Saturday night, May 11, 1963. A large crowd filled the stands, and some celebrities were there. Koufax allowed only two men on base and got five strikeouts. The fielders did the

Koufax *(center)* and fellow Dodgers' pitcher Don Drysdale *(right)* horse around with comedian Milton Berle (in Mets uniform) on the show *Hollywood Palace* in April 1966. Both pitchers had recently renewed their contracts with the Los Angeles Dodgers after protracted negotiations with the management. In spite of his spectacular success, Koufax shied away from the limelight so fans savored moments such as this where they saw him off the baseball field.

rest. But Koufax got the last out himself when the ball was hit towards the pitcher's mound. He grabbed the ball and threw the batter out at first. That was it! Koufax had pitched his second no-hitter! The stadium went wild!

Koufax had thrown a total of 112 pitches in that game. Afterward, he thanked his fielders and his catcher, John Roseboro, for the great

Koufax pitched four no-hitters in four years. Here he is caught in action against Philadelphia in the fifth inning of his third no-hitter. The Dodgers shut out the Phillies 3–0. Koufax struck out 12 players.

plays they made. Koufax later said that no one came near him in the dugout during the game. They were afraid they would jinx what, at the time, was looking like a possible shutout. Call it superstition, but it worked.

The excitement seemed to last all night. Koufax was congratulated by everyone he met. Koufax then traveled to the San Fernando Valley to do a children's fundraiser on a local radio station.

By the time the All-Star Game took place, Koufax had an ERA of 1.73 and had already tallied 150 strikeouts. He had achieved these numbers with fewer pitches than he had thrown before. His new goal, he said, was to make batters go after more of his pitches.

Sandy Koufax was on fire, and the baseball world took notice. He was at the top of his game with a 14–3 record. His finger seemed fine, and he no longer worried about a relapse. In fact, he thought that he had been misdiagnosed.

At the end of the 1963 season, the Dodgers had clinched the pennant. Koufax held incredible numbers. He had struck out 306 batters in

311 innings. His ERA was 1.88, once again topping the National League. The Dodgers would need him when they went up against the New York Yankees in the World Series.

The Underdogs

The Yankees were favored to win the World Series in 1963. Alston decided to start Koufax in Game 1, against Whitey Ford. Alston reasoned that if the Dodgers could win Game 1, they would still be in the standings.

At first Ford was able to match Koufax, keeping the game scoreless. But in the second inning the Dodgers started to put numbers on the board. Outfielder Frank Howard hit a double right over Mickey Mantle's head! Bill Skowron and Dick Tracewski each hit singles.

The bases were loaded when catcher John Roseboro stepped onto the plate. Keeping his eye on the ball, he blasted one into the crowd—a grand slam! The Dodgers were ahead 4–0!

In the third inning, the Dodgers scored again, giving Koufax a comfortable 5–0 lead. Eventually the Yankees scored, so Koufax did not get a shutout. But he was pleased with his performance. He had played with a cold and a sore elbow. He did what was needed for the Dodgers to win Game 1. And he had broken a World Series' record for strikeouts.

There were 69,000 fans in attendance that first game. Sixty-nine thousand fans watched Koufax strike out 15 Yankees and break the World Series record.

The record had been held by Dodgers' pitcher Carl Erskine, who had pitched 14 strikeouts during a game against the Yankees in 1939. Erskine had beaten the record held by Howard Ehmke. Playing for the Philadelphia Athletes, Ehmke had pitched a game with 13 strikeouts in 1929. It took twenty years for the record to be broken twice, and Koufax did it.

Game 2 belonged to Johnny Podres, the Dodgers' other left-handed pitcher. He pitched a great game, allowing only one run. The final score of Game 2 was 4–1, Dodgers.

Next it was Don Drysdale's turn. He was the Dodgers' right-handed pitcher. The Dodgers played this game in Los Angeles, where the fans

Koufax poses with teammates Ron Perranoski, Johnny Podres, and Don Drysdale on the eve of the opening match of the 1963 World Series against the New York Yankees. The game was played at Yankee Stadium, and Koufax struck out 15 Yankees on their home ground. Koufax went on to be named MVP of the series.

were excited to see that their team was up two games to none against the New York Yankees. Now the Dodgers had the home-field advantage. Drysdale came through, striking out nine players during that game to win it 1–0.

The Dodgers were ahead in the series, three games to nothing. Could they shut out the Yankees? It was in the hands of Sandy Koufax, who had been called to start Game 4.

Game 4, and the pressure was on. It was Koufax versus Ford and Ford versus Koufax. The Yankees needed to win this game to stay in the series. The Dodgers needed this win to take home the trophy.

Ford allowed only two hits during the game. Both hits belonged to Frank Howard. His second, in the fifth inning, was a home run. He gave the Dodgers a 1–0 lead.

Things were looking good for the Dodgers until Mickey Mantle hit one off of Koufax, to tie the score in the top of the seventh inning.

When the Dodgers came up to bat, Junior Gilliam hit a bouncing ball to third baseman Clete Boyer, who threw the ball to first. However, first baseman Joe Pepitone muffed Boyer's accurate throw, allowing Gilliam to reach third base.

Willie Davis, up next, hit the ball deep into center field. Mantle caught the ball and Gilliam tagged up. As Gilliam sprinted to the plate, Mantle fired the ball home. Gilliam beat out the throw, making the score 2–1.

Koufax is mobbed by his teammates after he clinches the fourth game in the 1963 World Series against the New York Yankees. The Dodgers shut out the Yankees 4–0 to win the World Series trophy.

In the ninth inning, the Yankees gave Koufax a run for his money. Tension was high. The tying run was on second base. Koufax pitched to Hector Lopez, who hit the ball toward the shortstop. The ball was thrown to first and the game was over. The Dodgers won the World Series in a shutout against the New York Yankees!

"Athlete of the Year"

Winning the 1963 World Series skyrocketed Koufax to fame. He was showered with honors and trophies. He was named the National League's Most Valuable Player by the Baseball Writers' Association of America (BBWAA). *The Sporting News* named him Player of the Year. The Associated Press honored him as Male Athlete of the Year. The BBWAA New York division presented him with the Babe Ruth Award as the most outstanding player in the World Series.

In Los Angeles, Fairfax Avenue was renamed Koufax Avenue! One of the biggest honors was the Cy Young Award, which is awarded to the best pitcher in baseball, one for the American League and one for the National League. Winning unanimously, Koufax was everybody's favorite!

The awards reinforced what Koufax's peers already knew. Now it seemed like everybody in baseball was trying to get their paws on Sandy. Baseball organizations and fans were coming out of the woodwork to get a little piece of Sandy Koufax. A little piece of baseball history!

1964—The Year of Injuries

The Dodgers began to take a turn for the worse in 1964, primarily due to injuries sustained by the players. Koufax was included in this list. He seemed to be hurting while he was on the mound. His elbow was inflamed, and his doctor feared that he had torn muscles in his arm. Koufax was sent to Los Angeles to meet with doctors. While there, Koufax underwent a series of treatments for his arm and elbow. Ice packs, hot whirlpool baths, and ultrasounds were part of the therapy. He was also given cortisone injections in the affected muscles.

In May, Koufax was put back into the game. Luckily for the Dodgers, he seemed to be back in form. In June, Koufax pitched the third no-hitter of his career, this time against the Philadelphia Phillies. In all of baseball history, only three other pitchers had accomplished such a feat. They were Larry Corcoran in 1880, 1882, and 1884; Cy Young in 1897, 1904, and 1908; and Bob Feller in 1940, 1946, and 1951.

The Cy Young Award

Cy Young was among the first American League superstar baseball pitchers. He won a total of 511 games in his career. That is nearly 100 more games than any other pitcher in baseball history!

Denton True "Cy" Young was born on March 29, 1867, in Gilmore, Ohio. He had his best season in 1901, leading in wins, strikeouts, and ERAs. Two years later, playing for Boston, he won two games in the first World Series, helping the Boston Pilgrims to become the first ever World Series winners! In 1937, "Cy" (short for cyclone) was inducted into the Baseball Hall of Fame by the Baseball Writers' Association of America.

Almost twenty years later, in 1956, baseball commissioner Ford Frick felt that pitchers didn't have enough chances to win the Most Valuable Player (MVP) Award. He wanted to create an honor for the best pitcher of every baseball season. Cy Young had passed away on November 4, 1955, so Frick named the award after him.

On July 9, 1956, the **BBWAA** established the Cy Young Memorial Award, which one pitcher would receive each year. One sportswriter from every major league baseball city would vote. In the case of a tie, a second vote would take place between the two competing pitchers.

In 1967, William Eckert, Frick's successor, approved a new rule that let two writers nominate a player from each league, resulting in an American and National League winner.

This worked until 1969, when Denny McLain and Mike Cuellar were tied for the American League award. To prevent a tie in the future, a points system was established. Every writer would now pick three pitchers from each league. Their first-choice player received five points. Their second-choice player received three points. Their third-choice player received one point. The nominee with the highest score wins.

There were a number of years when players were voted in unanimously. Some players have won this honor more than once.

Unanimous winners of the Cy Young Award		
1963	Sandy Koufax, NL	
1965	Sandy Koufax, NL	
1966	Sandy Koufax, NL	
1968	Bob Gibson, NL	
1968	Denny Mclain, AL	
1972	Steve Carlton, NL	
1978	Ron Guidry, AL	
1984	Rick Sutcliffe, NL	
1985	Dwight Gooden, NL	
1986	Roger Clemens, AL	
1988	Orel Hershiser, NL	
1994	Greg Maddux, NL	
1995	Greg Maddux, NL	

A benefit to this voting system is that it allows relievers to receive the award as well.

1974	Mike Marshall, NL	
1977	Sparky Lyle, AL	
1979	Bruce Sutter, NL	
1981	Rollie Fingers, AL	
1984	Willie Hernandez, AL	
1987	Steve Bedrosian, NL	
1989	Mark Davis, NL	
1992	Dennis Eckersley, AL	

Koufax pitched an incredible game. He struck out 12 batters in front of more than 29,000 fans. At twenty-eight years old, he was in a class all his own. When asked if he went into a game thinking he'd pitch a no-hitter, Sandy replied, "I guess a fellow starts thinking about the possibility of a no-hitter when he's finished warming up for a game. Every time I start I think of it. I know I'm not going to pitch one every time out but you never know if that first hit will beat you. . ."

The Helping Youth Award

Up next against Koufax and the Dodgers were the New York Mets. Before the game began, an award ceremony was held for Koufax. Members of his old Ice Cream League team, the Tomahawks, were there to honor him. Jimmy Murphy, one of the founders of the league, presented Koufax with the Helping Youth Award. He explained that Koufax was chosen for this award because the community recognized him as an athlete who spent some of his time with children.

In an August game against the Braves, Koufax injured his elbow sliding into second base. While he brushed it off and continued playing, a couple of games later the pain returned. The Dodgers decided to give him less playing time in the hopes that the down-time would help him heal.

By the end of August, he was sent back to Los Angeles. His doctors determined that the injury could not be repaired with quick medication and treatment. Instead, it would need time to heal.

Koufax did not return for that season. He said that if he had given the injury more time to heal after it initially happened, perhaps he could have prevented missing the rest of the season. But he had already won 19 games. He wanted his twentieth win, and that zeal made him stay in the game.

In December of that year, when contract negotiations were completed, Koufax and Drysdale had become the highest-paid baseball pitchers ever.

1965 and the Pain Returns

The 1965 spring training season in Vero Beach started out like many others. Koufax's stance on the mound looked good and his pitching was consistent. He looked at the beginning of the season as a chance to start anew. His goal was to break some of his earlier records. But this hope vaporized as he began to feel the pain in his elbow again. That April, his pitching coaches sent him back to the doctors in Los Angeles.

Dr. Robert Kerlan diagnosed Koufax with a traumatic arthritic condition in his elbow! Arthritis was chronic, which meant that it would be with him forever. The doctor didn't think Koufax would be back to play that season. Although arthritis does not have a cure, treatment could make Koufax's arm feel more comfortable. But how long would it last?

The repeat motions of his pitches eventually caused pain to his arm. For one week Koufax underwent treatment similar to the previous year—shots of cortisone in the arm, heat, and massage. In the meantime, the Dodgers acquired another left-handed pitcher named Claude Osteen for backup in case Koufax could not return.

Koufax was back on the mound by April 18. He managed to strike out seven men against Philadelphia, and the Dodgers won 6–2. When asked if he felt a difference or if he was purposely doing something in a new way, Koufax answered, "I'm cutting out the sidearming because I want to eliminate irritation because it may have been what brought on the arthritis in the first place." When asked when he felt most afflicted by the pain, he said that it mostly happened when he was asleep. The pain woke him up!

Surprisingly, the elbow and the arthritis behaved. Koufax was able to pitch, although at times he was a little shaky. The quality of his pitching depended on how inflamed his arm was when he woke up in the morning.

Well into July, Koufax was still in the rotation. Up to this point, he had pitched 14 complete games out of 21 starts. He had earned 169 strikeouts. This was normal for him, but it would be exceptional for any other pitcher. In order to

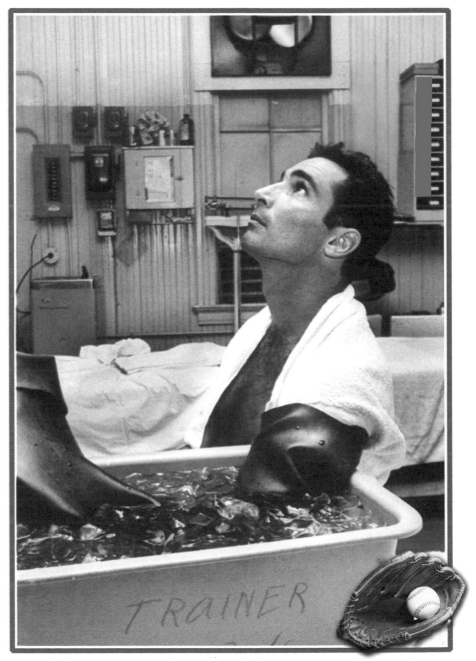

Koufax eases the pain and inflammation in his throwing arm by immersing his elbow in a bucket of ice after a game against the New York Mets in 1966.

achieve his numbers, his arm was watched very carefully. He was examined after every game. The doctors checked for excessive inflammation.

Koufax's arm was massaged between innings. After games, he wrapped his left arm in either a sleeve of cellophane or a piece of an inner tube. Then be dipped his arm into a bucket of ice. He soaked it for long periods of time. The rubber inner tube prevented Koufax from getting frostbite on his arm. He was also required to take capsules that contained buta-zolidin alka, an anti-inflammatory. He took these pills once before the day he pitched, once the morning of the game, and once on the day after he pitched.

Koufax was willing to endure this daily reg-imen. He was at the top of his game again. By August, he had 19 wins under his belt. At this pace, there was a good chance he could break the record for the number of games won by a pitcher, a record that had been held by Dizzy Dean since 1934—the year before Koufax was born!

The Perfect Game

September 10, 1965, went down in baseball history. It was the day Sandy Koufax became the eighth pitcher to pitch a perfect game! He did it against the Chicago Cubs at Dodgers Stadium, in front of a crowd of 29,000 fans. He struck out 14 of the 27 batters he faced. His toughest moment came in the eighth inning when was up against the Cubs' two toughest hitters, Ernie Banks and Ron Santo. It didn't last long. Koufax struck them out! Then he easily eliminated their rookie left fielder, Bryon Browne.

In the final inning, Chris Krug was at the plate with a count of two balls and two strikes. Koufax looked toward home, nodded to his catcher, and threw a fastball down the middle. Krug didn't have a chance! He was out.

Next, Joe Amalfitano took his place at the plate. His first pitch was a strike! One out, with the score at 1–0 at the bottom of the ninth, one strike on Amalfitano. Koufax pitched. Amalfitano got a piece of the ball and fouled it. Koufax fired another fastball down the middle of the plate and got him!

With two away, Harvey Kuenn was next at bat. He swung at a fastball for strike one. Koufax threw a high, wild pitch to Kuenn. Ball one.

Koufax composed himself on the mound and fired a fastball. It was high, for ball two. Again, Koufax took a moment at the mound, readied himself, and threw. Kuenn swung and missed. Strike two. The count was now two balls and two strikes, with two outs. The fans were on their feet. Koufax delivered a pitch. Kuenn took a swing. Strike three! The crowd went wild!

Sandy Koufax had just pitched his fourth no-hitter!

Sandy Koufax had just pitched a PERFECT GAME! He had made baseball history!

Koufax *(number 32)* is congratulated by teammates after pitching a perfect game against the Chicago Cubs in 1965. The Dodgers won 1–0.

The Stats Say It All

This perfect game also made Koufax the only pitcher to have pitched four no-hitters. That meant that he threw a no-hitter once every season for four seasons straight! He broke other records, too. He struck out 382 batters that season, setting a new major league record. He won the most games in the National League with 26, and he had an ERA of 2.04. In his career, Koufax pitched an incredible 3,352.3 innings.

Major League Baseball Perfect Games

Year	Name, Team	Game	Date	Score
1880	J. Richmond, Worchester	vs. Cleveland	June 12	1–0
1904	Cy Young, Boston	vs. Philadelphia	June 17	5–0
1908	Addie Joss, Cleveland	vs. Chicago	Oct. 2	1–0
1917	Ernie Shore, Boston	vs. Washington	June 23	4–0
1922	C.C. Robertson, Chicago	vs. Detroit	April 30	2–0
1956	Don Larsen, New York	vs. Brooklyn	Oct. 8	2–0
1964	Jim Bunning, Philadelphia	vs. New York	June 21	6–0
1965	Sandy Koufax, Los Angeles	vs. Chicago	Sept. 10	1–0

A Controversial Decision

The Dodgers continued to win, working their way to the play-offs. They had to beat Milwaukee to get into the World Series that year. Koufax pitched the third game of the play-off series. He got his twenty-sixth win of the season with a record-breaking 382 strikeouts. The Dodgers were once again going to the World Series!

Game 1 against Minnesota was scheduled for Wednesday, October 6. It happened that Yom Kippur fell on that day in 1965. This was a conflict for Koufax because Yom Kippur was a Jewish High Holy Day, the day of Atonement.

On Yom Kippur, observant Jews spend the day in temple reflecting on the year and contemplating how to become better people. Starting at sundown, many Jews fast to cleanse their souls of their sins.

Koufax decided not to pitch on Yom Kippur. Instead, he would go to temple. This decision became historic as well as controversial. Rabbis applauded his decision. They felt that there was finally a good sports role model for the young children of their congregations. Baseball fans and members of the media argued that it showed a lack of loyalty toward his occupation. Koufax had to endure nasty anti-Semitic comments. Some argued that if he really loved baseball, he would not let his religion get in his way.

But Koufax stood his ground. He explained that he had decided long ago that baseball would not interfere with his religious beliefs. As a teen player, he once asked a coach what he should do when a similar situation arose. The coach had told Sandy then to do what he thought was the right thing, regardless of what others said. From that day forward, Sandy Koufax always followed that advice.

The 1965 World Series

The Dodgers knew they were up against heavy-hitters on the Minnesota team. The Twins led the American League in hitting. The Dodgers were known to have a strong pitching staff to back up their weak hitters. This contrast would make for an interesting series.

Don Drysdale, replacing Koufax, pitched Game 1. The Twins showed him a lot of hitting muscle and won the game 8–2, including a crushing three-run homer from the Twins' Zoilo Versalles.

Dodgers fans hoped Koufax would do better in Game 2. Unfortunately, they did not get their wish. The Minnesota Twins beat Koufax and the Dodgers, 5–1. Koufax allowed two runs and the Dodgers' outfielders made errors throughout the game.

Some people attributed Koufax's weak pitching to the mound in Bloomington Stadium, which they claimed was lower than the mound at Dodgers Stadium. Koufax did not buy this; he simply said that his control was off and that there was nothing more to it. He had also been complaining to teammates that he was extremely tired. The wear and tear on his elbow may have had a bigger effect than even he realized.

Game 3 was played back at Dodgers Stadium. Claude Osteen, the left-hander, who had been added to the Dodgers' pitching staff when Koufax was having his medical problems, was on the roster to start. Fans and critics alike must have been thinking that if Koufax and Drysdale couldn't beat the Twins, then how could Osteen, a backup pitcher, do the job?

Osteen surprised everyone, and the Dodgers beat the Twins 4–0. Being a modest pitcher, Osteen said that he was simply trying to get the batters to hit the ball in the ground. He knew he didn't have Koufax's speed or the ability to overpower them like Drysdale, so he used what he had.

Drysdale was back on the mound for Game 4 of the series. Having won a game, the Dodgers had a renewed sense of confidence. With the series at 2–1, it was anybody's game. Defensively, Drysdale allowed five hits and struck out 11 batters. The Dodgers offense looked good as the players rounded the bases with walks and steals. The final score was 7–2, in favor of the Dodgers.

Keeping with the rotation, Koufax was up next for Game 5. The series was tied, creating a new momentum for both teams. Fans could feel the excitement in the air. Koufax pitched an incredible game, shutting out Minnesota, 7–0. Having allowed only four hits, he had struck out 10 batters, more than making up for the last game he pitched. This win became the eighty-fourth time he had struck out 10 or more batters in a game.

As usual, he had the highest pitching record in the National League. Considering how poorly he had been feeling, Koufax thought he had played pretty well. "I was surprised they didn't get more hits. My control

Koufax unwinds and is about to release the ball in the final game of the 1965 World Series against the Minnesota Twins. The Dodgers took home the trophy and Koufax won his second World Series MVP.

wasn't sharp and I got awfully tired toward the end," he said afterward, as reported by Jerry Mitchell in his book *Sandy Koufax*.

The two teams flew back to Minnesota to finish off the series. Minnesota felt confident that with the home-field advantage they would win. There may have been some wisdom in this belief because the Twins did take Game 6. Pitcher Mudcat Grant allowed six hits and hit a home run in the sixth inning. The final score was 5–1. The series was now three wins for the Twins and two wins for the Dodgers. Game 7 would determine the winner of the 1965 World Series.

Twins' manager Sam Mele announced that Jim Kaat would pitch for them. Alston, on the other hand, could not decide between using Koufax or Drysdale. He wanted to start a left-handed pitcher. Both men had at least two days of rest. When Alston asked them, each said he'd be happy with whatever decision was made.

Alston met with his players the morning of the game and asked them whom they thought should start the game. In the end, he chose Koufax, and Koufax did not disappoint. Pitching an amazing game, he shut out the Twins, 2–0.

The Dodgers had won the World Series! A hush fell over the 50,000-plus Minnesota fans as they watched Koufax defeat each batter at the plate. When the last out was made, the Dodgers went into their clubhouse to celebrate.

Koufax was satisfied with a job well done. Pleased that the season was over and that he could rest his arm, he planned to reward himself with a vacation to Hawaii.

Koufax was named the 1965 World Series Most Valuable Player. His achievments were reinforced when he was unanimously nominated for the Cy Young Award for the second time. He had managed to break records in both the American and National Leagues. With a phenomenal 382 strikeouts, he broke a record that had stood for nineteen years. Robert Feller of the Chicago Cubs held the record at 348.

Koufax poses with the Cy Young Award honoring him as best pitcher in both leagues of major league baseball in 1966.

Koufax's Numbers in 1965

Wins: 26
Innings pitched: 336
Strikeouts: 382
ERA: 2.04

That fall, Sandy Koufax attended many dinners and award ceremonies in his honor. He was awarded the $10,000 Hickok Belt as the Professional Athlete of the Year. This was the second time he received this award, and it was the first time in the award's history that it was given to the same person twice.

He also received the Van Heusen Outstanding Achievement Award for the second time. Other awards included the Mercer Award and the Ruth Award, which he had won the previous year. First-time honors given to him were the Sid Mercer Memorial (Player of the Year) and the Babe Ruth World Series Star Award.

Sandy Koufax Retires

Koufax had another strong season in 1966. He was one of baseball's highest-paid pitchers. His pitching record was 27 wins and nine loses. He recorded his best ERA, 1.73. Koufax also tallied an incredible total of 317 strikeouts. When he was awarded his third Cy Young Award, no one was surprised. He was the first pitcher to receive this award three times. Koufax was at the top of his game.

It's Time

On November 18, 1966, at a press conference at the Regent Beverly Wiltshire Hotel in Los Angeles, Sandy Koufax announced his retirement. He was only thirty years old. There were mixed reactions. Reporters applauded him knowing that he had a good run. Women cried.

Koufax announces his retirement at a press conference in 1966 after pitching only 12 years in the majors. Sandy said, "I don't regret for one minute the 12 years I've spent in baseball, but I could regret one season too many." In his career, he made six all-star appearances and won three Cy Young Awards and two World Series MVP awards.

The baseball world was in shock. Sandy had just pitched his best season, clinching the pennant for Los Angeles for the second straight year. He was on a roll. Why quit now?

Koufax explained that the arthritis in his left arm was causing some serious symptoms. There were days when Koufax couldn't straighten his arm anymore. His clothes had to be altered to make the left sleeve shorter. He had to bend his neck to get his face to his left arm when he shaved. When the pain was really bad, he'd shave with his right hand. Even during some meals, it was a challenge for him to hold his utensils. He'd have to move closer to his plate.

When he was playing baseball, he had to take a variety of anti-inflammatory drugs before and after games. These drugs upset his stomach. They also slowed down his reaction time so much that he feared he would get hit by a line drive.

To bring down the swelling after a game, Sandy had to soak his arm in a bucket of ice water after wrapping it in an inner tube to prevent it from getting frostbite. His doctors told him that doing all this might allow him to continue playing baseball, but it could not prevent permanent damage to his left arm. Some doctors had said there was a possibility that he would lose complete use of his arm. That's why it was time for Sandy to retire from baseball.

Baseball Commentator

Sandy Koufax became a television commentator for the NBC television network shortly after he retired from pitching, signing a ten-year contract. He talked about the pitchers in the televised games, easily naming and describing each pitch.

Fellow commentators insisted on comparing the pitchers to Koufax, which made him feel uncomfortable. He would avoid talking about himself whenever he could. Koufax broke his contract after six years, in February 1973.

Anne Widmark

In 1968, Koufax met Anne Widmark. She was in Malibu, California, redecorating her parents' summer home when Koufax spotted her and offered to help her paint. He didn't tell her about himself. Later, she discovered who he was and he found out that she was the daughter of the actor Richard Widmark. Anne and Sandy fell in love and were married six months later. A private ceremony was held at her father's home in West Los Angeles with fewer than twenty guests.

Koufax capped a brilliant career as a pitcher with a stretch of sportscasting on the NBC television network.

Winkumpaugh Farm

When Koufax turned thirty-five years old, he decided he wanted to move from Los Angeles, where he and Anne were living, to a quieter, more private location. One day he came across a magazine article that described a small, sleepy town in Maine. The article featured an old Cape-style farmhouse called Winkumpaugh Farm. One of Anne's friends was renovating her farmhouse in Maine so Sandy decided to take a look at it.

Winkumpaugh Farm was owned by Blakely and Alberta Babcock. It was surrounded by beautiful landscaping. The Koufaxes fell in love with Winkumpaugh Farm. On October 4, 1971, Sandy and Anne Koufax took out a mortgage and bought the farmhouse.

Koufax built a sound system that ran throughout the house. He became a gourmet cook, and the couple threw many parties. But Koufax liked to keep his parties private and intimate and he never invited big celebrities. Eventually, he purchased 300 acres of land surrounding his farmhouse to add to his privacy.

Golf

Koufax also took up golf. He often played at the Bucksport Golf Club in Maine. It was a modest club where there were no signs that said Members Only. Members parked their own cars. The club featured a nine-hole course. Golfers played the white tees for the first nine holes, and the blue tees for the last nine.

In 1973, Koufax decided to play in the Maine State Amateur Tournament. He had become a passionate golfer.

In the game of golf, a player must complete each hole within a certain number of shots, called "par." A golfer's handicap is the number of shots over par within a game. One day, while working on a tractor, an idea came to Sandy. He created a grip on his club that would allow him to lessen his handicap to six.

He entered the tournament and advanced to the final round. After making a 30-foot putt onto the eighteenth hole, he missed sinking the ball and lost. He had been just one shot away from the championship!

Leaving Maine

By the summer of 1974, Koufax decided he had had enough of the cold Maine winters. His farmhouse required a lot of maintenance, and his stepfather, who lived in California, was ill. Koufax sold his farm and moved to Templeton, California.

Baseball, the Second Time Around

In 1979, Koufax began a new job with the Los Angeles Dodgers. Until then, his only income came from card show appearances, where he was paid to sign autographs for fans. He had never wanted to accept the fruitful sports endorsements that so many athletes rely on for extra income. So when the Dodgers asked him to come back as a roving minor league pitching coach, he accepted.

This job gave him the chance to travel to towns in the United States such as San Antonio, Texas; Albuquerque, New Mexico; and Great Falls, Montana. He talked with pitchers and helped them perfect their techniques.

Pitching legend Sandy Koufax gives a few tips to the Dodgers' Mike Trombley during spring training in February 2002.

The young players loved Koufax. They thought his teaching style was clean, stylish, and understated. They loved the little secrets he taught them. Orel Hershiser, a former Dodger, removed some of the spikes on the back of his right shoe, allowing him to push off the pitcher's mound like Koufax had done. Dwight Gooden and Chun Ho Park were students of his curveball. To this day, Mets' closer John Franco insists that he couldn't master Koufax's overhand curveball. Franco thought his fingers were too short. Koufax's long, slender fingers had made him the king of curveballs. By placing his thumb on the top of the ball as a guide, he was able to snap it by pulling down as he released the ball.

Koufax came to the aid of a certain pitcher the league considered a hothead. It was Koufax who stood up for him, warning the management that they would be turning away "the best arm on the staff." This player, John Wetteland, a Texas Rangers' closer, was in his eleventh year of baseball at the time this book was written.

Koufax left his coaching job in February of 1990 as a result of a misunderstanding with Dodgers' owner Peter O'Malley. O'Malley instructed the farm director to lessen Koufax's work assignments. He thought he was giving the superstar a break. Koufax, on the other hand, took offense at this move. He convinced himself that he was getting paid for doing nothing. Being a proud person, Koufax quit.

A Marriage Ends, Another Begins

Sandy and Anne Koufax were divorced in the early 1980s. A few years later, Koufax met and married a woman with a passion for the arts. They moved to Oregon, where she managed an art gallery. They also bought a home in North Carolina, where they kept horses. This marriage ended in the 1990s. Koufax has remained on his own ever since. His friends have reported that Koufax enjoys his time alone and being able to do whatever he likes.

Koufax *(left)* jokes with Ed Junker *(center)*, former head coach of the University of Cincinnati's basketball team.

Spring Training

In 1993, Kevin Kennedy, a baseball analyst who was once the manager of the Texas Rangers, asked Koufax to join the team at spring training. Koufax accepted, but for one week only. He wore an unmarked jersey because he felt it was best to keep a low profile. During the day, he watched the team play and offered advice. At night, he dined with pitching coach Claude Osteen. For hours, they talked baseball. Koufax had a great time.

The New York Mets' Al Leiter is one of the younger generation of pitchers who have benefited from Koufax's advice.

Mets' Camp

In 2001, Koufax visited the New York Mets' camp. Owner Fred Wilpon, who had been a teammate at Lafayette High School in Brooklyn, and Mets pitching coach Dave Wallace, asked Koufax to speak to the players. In the locker room, he talked to the crowd, telling left-hander Al Leiter that he played really well and that he could be even better. When Leiter asked for help, Koufax showed him how to improve his aim at the plate.

Koufax also explained how to pitch more defensively when a right-hander was at bat. Leiter, who received some priceless advice, values his friendship with Koufax. Leiter has said that after talking to Koufax, he had the best season of his career, with 17 wins and six losses. He believes that Koufax really did help him to become a better player.

Koufax's Division

The American Amateur Baseball Congress (AABC) was founded in 1935. It is the largest amateur baseball organization for young baseball players in the United States. Comprised of seven divisions divided by age groups, the divisions are located in the United States, as well as in Puerto Rico and Canada.

The Sandy Koufax Division is for players ages fourteen and under. When a team wins its state tournament, it advances to a regional game. Regional winners play in the Sandy Koufax World Series. The 2001 Sandy Koufax World Series was held in Jersey City, New Jersey. The Texas Tigers of Dallas was the winning team.

The Baseball Hall of Fame

Baseball was invented in 1839 in an upstate New York town called Cooperstown. In the beginning, the game was called town ball. Twenty to fifty boys stood in a street. The "tosser" would hit the ball into the field using a four-inch flat bat. What was the object of this game? To catch the ball!

Abner Graves and Abner Doubleday were schoolmates in Cooperstown. Graves claimed that Doubleday made changes to town ball, which included drawing a diamond-shaped field in the dirt, adding bases at each point of the diamond, and adding a pitcher and a catcher. Doubleday renamed the sport baseball.

This is a portrait of Abner Doubleday, a Union general in the U.S. Civil War, who is credited with having invented baseball. Many, however, dispute this claim.

A committee of seven was appointed in 1905 to determine the accuracy of this claim. It was headed by Albert G. Spalding and Henry Chadwick. Spalding had received letters from his friend, Abner Graves, describing Dou-

This is a picture of the first ball believed to have been used to play baseball.

bleday's changes. On December 30, 1907, it was declared that Abner Doubleday had created baseball in 1839 in Cooperstown, New York.

In 1934, Abner Graves's belongings were found in an old farmhouse in Fly Creek, New York, three miles away from Cooperstown. Included in the discovery was a homemade baseball. It was lopsided, torn open, and stuffed with cloth. The cover of the ball had been stitched together, like the baseballs we know today.

A Cooperstown man named Stephen C. Clark bought the first baseball for five dollars. He began a collection of baseball objects and created an exhibition in a room of the Village Club. The exhibit became a popular attraction, drawing

Sandy Koufax was inducted into the Baseball Hall of Fame *(pictured above)* in 1972.

visitors from all over the world. With the help of his colleague Alexander Cleland, Clark introduced the idea of a national baseball museum.

Donations and baseball memorabilia came in from around the country. It was decided that the Hall of Fame would be opened in 1939, to coincide with the 100-year anniversary of baseball. The Hall of Fame would be part of a shrine to honor the people involved with the national pastime.

On June 12, 1939, the National Baseball Hall of Fame was officially dedicated in a ribbon-cutting ceremony. Some of the first inductees were Ty Cobb, Babe Ruth, Honus Wagner, Christy Mathewson, and Walter Johnson. Of the 25 players who were inducted, 11 were still alive. They all attended the ceremony at the Cooperstown post office. A special baseball stamp was issued to commemorate the event.

Attendance at the Hall of Fame now reaches close to 400,000 each year. The busiest months are July and August. The most popular annual event is Hall of Fame Day, when there is a ceremony for new inductees. The sport of baseball has won the hearts of many Americans.

Koufax's Big Day

Sandy Koufax was inducted into the National Baseball Hall of Fame on August 12, 1972. At the age of thirty-six, he was the youngest player ever inducted. His baseball statistics were amazing. He had led the National League in

ERAs for five years. His lifetime ERA was an impressive 2.76. In terms of strikeouts, he was at the top of the game, leading the league for four seasons. Three out of those four years, he struck out over 300 batters. With a lifetime winning percentage of .655, and 165 wins and 87 losses, he averaged more than a strikeout per inning!

In addition to his awesome statistics, Koufax was a great strategic player on the mound. He could outsmart many batters by alternating pitches. When he wanted to show them who was boss, he went in for the kill with a fastball. Willie Stargell is reported to have said, "Hitting against Sandy Koufax is like eating soup with a fork!"

He was in good company when he was inducted into the Hall of Fame. That year, the other inductees included Luke Appling, Yogi Berra, Lou Boudreau, Roy Campanella, Earle Combs, Stan Coveleski, Joe Cronin, Bill Dickey, Bob Feller, Ford Frick, Frank Frisch, Charlie Gehringer, Lefty Gomez, Lefty Grove, Chick Hafey, Jesse Haines, Harry Hooper,

Koufax's Career Pitching Record

Year	Team	G	W	L	PCT	ERA	IP	H	BB	SO
1955	Brooklyn	12	2	2	.500	3.02	41.2	33	28	30
1956	Brooklyn	16	2	4	.333	4.91	58.2	66	29	30
1957	Brooklyn	34	5	4	.556	3.88	104.1	83	51	122
1958	LA	40	11	11	.500	4.48	158.2	132	105	131
1959	LA	35	8	6	.571	4.05	153.1	136	92	173
1960	LA	37	8	13	.381	3.91	175	133	100	197
1961	LA	42	18	13	.581	3.52	255.2	212	96	269
1962	LA	28	14	7	.667	2.54	184.1	134	57	216
1963	LA	40	25	5	.833	1.88	311	214	58	306
1964	LA	29	19	5	.792	1.74	223	154	53	223
1965	LA	43	26	8	.765	2.04	335.2	216	71	382
1966	LA	41	27	9	.750	1.73	323	241	77	317
	Total	**397**	**165**	**87**	**.655**	**2.76**	**2,324.1**	**1,754**	**817**	**2,396**

G = Games, W = Wins, L = Losses, PCT = Win Percentage, ERA = Earned Run Average, IP = Innings Pitched, H = Hits allowed, BB = Bases on Balls, SO = Strikeouts

Waite Hoyt, Buck Leonard, Rube Marquard, Joe Medwick, Stan Musial, Sam Rice, Casey Stengel, Lloyd Waner, and Early Wynn.

A veterans' committee was created to allow Hall of Famers to vote for future members. There are 60 players on this committee. They meet for meals and go over Hall of Fame procedures.

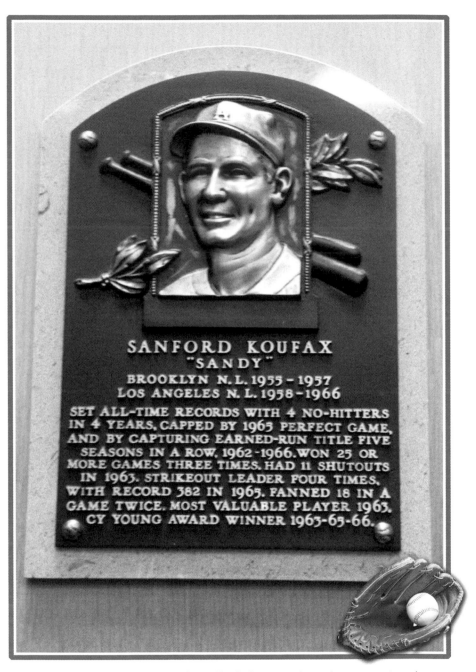

SANFORD KOUFAX
"SANDY"
BROOKLYN N.L. 1955 - 1957
LOS ANGELES N.L. 1958 - 1966
SET ALL-TIME RECORDS WITH 4 NO-HITTERS
IN 4 YEARS, CAPPED BY 1965 PERFECT GAME,
AND BY CAPTURING EARNED-RUN TITLE FIVE
SEASONS IN A ROW, 1962 - 1966. WON 25 OR
MORE GAMES THREE TIMES. HAD 11 SHUTOUTS
IN 1963. STRIKEOUT LEADER FOUR TIMES,
WITH RECORD 382 IN 1965. FANNED 18 IN A
GAME TWICE. MOST VALUABLE PLAYER 1963.
CY YOUNG AWARD WINNER 1963-65-66.

This plaque commemorates Sandy Koufax's outstanding achievements in and contributions to the game of baseball. It hangs in the Baseball Hall of Fame in Cooperstown, New York.

Conclusion

Although he has lived in many cities throughout his life, at this writing, Koufax has now settled in Vero Beach, Florida, where he is near the Dodgers' spring training camp. For the most part, he is a very private person. He makes appearances at card shows twice a year to sign autographs. He attends baseball games and other functions, but exits quietly to avoid the media.

Sandy Koufax's story is one of hard work and triumph. Perhaps his early injuries caused his career to end too soon. Nonetheless, he made the most out of his time on the mound. Koufax has often wondered aloud about his career. If he had played longer in the minor leagues at the beginning, would he have improved sooner? When he finally got his rhythm and was able to perfect his pitching, he became what many people consider the fastest pitcher in baseball. No one could get past his fastballs. Koufax is said to have no regrets. In only twelve years, he created plenty of records to challenge future pitchers.

After all, he is a baseball hall of famer.

SANDY KOUFAX *TIMELINE*

⚾	**Dec. 30 1935**	Sandy Koufax is born in Brooklyn, New York.
⚾	**Summer 1954**	Koufax signs as a "bonus baby" with the Brooklyn Dodgers.
⚾	**Aug. 27 1955**	In two consecutive games, Koufax gets a total of 23 strikeouts to tie the record at the time.
⚾	**Aug. 31 1959**	Koufax breaks Dizzy Dean's National League record and ties Bob Feller's record with 18 strikeouts in a game against the Giants.
⚾	**Sept. 15 1961**	Koufax throws 243 strikeouts, the most for a National League left-handed pitcher.
⚾	**June 30 1962**	Koufax pitches his first no-hitter against the New York Mets. The score is 5–0.
⚾	**July 17 1962**	The first of Koufax's injuries, a circulatory problem, causes him to be sidelined for the rest of the season.
⚾	**May 11 1963**	Koufax returns to the mound and delivers his second no-hitter against the Giants. The score is 8–0.
⚾	**Oct. 6 1963**	After the Dodgers win the first three games of the World Series against the New York Yankees, Koufax pitches Game 4 and completes the sweep.
⚾	**Oct. 24 1963**	Koufax unanimously wins the Cy Young Award.

	June 4 1964	Koufax gets his third no-hitter, against the Philadelphia Phillies. The score is 3–0.
	Aug. 16 1964	Koufax injures his elbow while sliding into second base. He misses the rest of the season.
	Sept. 10 1965	Koufax gets his fourth no-hitter in a perfect game against the Chicago Cubs. He becomes the eighth pitcher in baseball history to do so.
	Oct. 14 1965	Koufax pitches against the Minnesota Twins in the World Series and triumphs. It is the second World Series win for the Dodgers. Koufax is named the World Series Most Valuable Player.
	Feb.–Mar. 1966	Seeking to split $1.5 million, Koufax and Don Drysdale refuse to sign their contracts. They settle for $130,000 and $105,000, respectively.
	Sept. 29 1966	In three seasons, Koufax strikes out more than 300 batters. He is the first pitcher to do this since Amos Rusie in 1890–1892.
	Nov. 1 1966	Koufax becomes the first player to receive three Cy Young Awards.
	Nov. 18 1966	Koufax announces his retirement from major league baseball. His decision is a result of the increasing pain in his left elbow.
	Jan. 19 1972	The Baseball Writers' Association of America (BBWAA) nominates Sandy Koufax for membership into the National Baseball Hall of Fame. At age thirty-six, he is the youngest inductee.

Glossary

arthritis An inflammation of the joints.

change-up A tricky pitch that is thrown like a fastball but slows as it reaches the batter.

clinch When a team is guaranteed a spot in the World Series because it exceeds the number of wins needed in its division.

curveball A pitch that begins straight and curves to the right or the left of the plate.

Cy Young Award The highest honor given to pitchers in each baseball season. It is named after Cy Young, a record-breaking pitcher who played in the early 1900s.

earned run average (ERA) The average number of runs pitchers allow every nine innings they pitch. Runs scored due to errors are not counted in this average.

fastball The fastest pitch a pitcher can throw.

no-hitter A game when a pitcher doesn't allow any batters to get on base through hits.

Most Valuable Player (MVP)   A player who is voted top in the game in offensive and defensive playing. Conduct on the field is also considered.

perfect game   A game when the pitcher allows no one to reach first base.

pitch   The motion of throwing a baseball over home plate.

pitcher's mound   The raised area in the middle of the baseball diamond.

shutout   A game in which one team fails to score.

sweep   To win all the games in a series.

World Series   A number of games played between one American League and one National League baseball team to determine the championship team of the season. The winner must win four games out of seven.

Yom Kippur   A Jewish holiday observed with fasting and inner reflection. It is considered the most important holiday in the Jewish calendar.

For More Information

Baseball Almanac
11400 SW 40th Terrace
Miami, FL 33165-4605
Web site: http://www.baseball-almanac.com

CBS Sports
666 Third Avenue, 18th Floor
New York, NY 10017
(646) 487-1000
Web site: http://cbs.sportsline.com/u/
baseball/mlb/bol/koufax.htm

The Center for Jewish History
15 West 16th Street
New York, NY 10011
(212) 294-8301
Web site: http://www.yap.cat.nyu.edu/
jewsinsports/profile.asp?sport=
baseball&ID=5

Jewish Virtual Library
2810 Blaine Drive
Chevy Chase, MD 20815
(301) 565-3918
Web site: http://www.us-israel.org/jsource/
    biography/Koufax.html

Jews In Sports Online
Collaboration of the American Jewish
    Historic Society
15 West 16th Street
New York, NY 10011
(212) 294-6160
Web site: http://www.yap.cat.nyu.edu/
    jewsinsports/

National Baseball Hall of Fame and Museum
25 Main Street
P.O. Box 590
Cooperstown, NY 13326
(888) 425-5633
Web site: http://www.baseballhalloffame.org

For Further Reading

De Bourbon, Caucus. *Sandy Koufax*. San
Diego, CA: Revolutionary Comics, 1992.

Grabowski, John. *Sandy Koufax* (Baseball
Legends). New York: Chelsea House Publishing, 1992.

Gruver, Ed. *Koufax*. Dallas, TX: Taylor
Publishing Co., 2000.

Hano, A. *Sandy Koufax Strikeout King*.
New York: G.P. Putnam's Sons, 1966.

Mitchell, Jerry. *Sandy Koufax*. New York:
Tempo Books, 1966.

Sanford, William, and Carl K. Green. *Sandy
Koufax* (Sports Immortals). Boston, MA:
The Horn Book Inc., 1994.

Sloate, Susan. *Hotshots! Baseball Greats of
the Game When They Were Kids*. New York:
Sports Illustrated for Kids, 1991.

Bibliography

Brody, "Sy" Seymour. The Jewish Virtual
Library. "Sandy Koufax." Retrieved
November 2001 (http://www.us-israel.
org/jsource/biography/Koufax.html).

CBS Sports. "Sandy Koufax from the
Ballplayers." Retrieved December
2001 (http://cbs.sportsline.com/
u/baseball/mlb/ bol/koufax.htm).

Grabowski, John. *Sandy Koufax*
(Baseball Legends). New York:
Chelsea House Publishers, 1992.

Kramer, S.A. *Baseball's Greatest Pitchers*.
New York: Random House, 1992.

Mitchell, Jerry. *Sandy Koufax*. New York:
Tempo Books, 1966.

Schwartz, Larry. ESPN Classics. "Total
Domination." Retrieved December 2001

(http://www.espn.go.com/classic/
biography/s/koufaxsandyadd.html).
Sports Placement. "The Left Arm of God."
July 1999. Retrieved November 2001
(http://www.sportsplacement.com/
koufax2.htm).

Index

A

Alou, Felipe, 43
Alston, Walter (Dodgers' manager), 19, 26, 30–31, 34, 43, 73–74
Amalfitano, Joe, 65
American Amateur Baseball Congress (AABC), 90
Anderson, Wayne (Dodgers' trainer), 40
architecture, 12, 21
Ashburn, Richie, 36

B

Babe Ruth Award, 54, 76
Banks, Ernie, 64
Baseball Hall of Fame, 5, 94–97
baseball scouts, 15
Becker, Joe (Dodgers' pitching coach), 20, 34, 43
Berle, Milton, 44
Black, Joe, 19
Boyer, Clete, 52
Braun, Evelyn (mother), 9
Braun, Jack (father), 9
Brooklyn, New York, 9, 12
Browne, Byron, 64

C

Campanella, Roy, 19, 96
Camp Chi-Wan-Da, 14
Chicago Cubs, 26, 64, 74
Chicago White Sox, 30
Corcoran, Larry, 55
curveballs, 34–35, 40, 86
Cy Young Awards, 5, 7, 54, 74, 77

D

Davenport, Jim, 44
Davis, Willie, 44
Dodgers, 15–16, 24–25, 48–51, 55, 58–60, 67, 69, 71, 84
Drysdale, Don, 32, 44, 50, 59, 70–71, 73

E

earned run average (ERA), 24, 26, 33, 48, 66, 77, 96
Ehmke, Howard, 50
elbow injury, 7, 55, 59–63
Erskine, Carl, 50

F

fastballs, 25, 35, 41, 43, 65, 96
Feller, Bob, 28–30, 55, 74, 96
Ford, Whitey, 49, 52

G

Gilliam, Junior, 30, 52
golf, 83
Gooden, Dwight, 86

H

Helping Youth Award, 58
Hershiser, Orel, 86
Hicock Belt, 76
Howard, Frank, 44, 49, 52

I

Ice Cream League, 11, 58

J

Johnson, Walter, 30, 95

K

Kennedy, Kevin, 88
Koufax, Edith (stepsister), 9
Koufax, Irving (stepfather), 9, 84
Krug, Chris, 64
Kuenn, Harvey, 65

L

Lafayette High School, 12, 89
Leiter, Al, 89–90
Lopez, Hector, 53

M

Mantle, Mickey, 49, 52
Mauch, Gene (Phillies' manager), 28
Mays, Willie, 43
Mercer Award, 76
Milwaukee Braves, 22, 30, 67
Minnesota Twins, 69, 72–74
Moon, Wally, 30
Murphy, Jimmy, 58

N

National League, 49, 66, 71, 95–96
    Most Valuable Player, 54
    pitching record, 22, 28–29, 33
New York Giants, 15, 30
New York Mets, 35–36, 58, 89
New York Yankees, 49–51, 53
no-hitters, 36–37, 45, 55, 58, 65–66

O

O'Malley, Peter (Dodgers' owner), 87
Osteen, Claude, 61, 70, 88

P

Park, Chun Ho, 86
Pepitone, Joe, 52
perfect game, 7, 36, 65–66
Perranoski, Ron, 43
Philadelphia Phillies, 55
Pittsburgh Pirates, 15, 22
Player of the Year, 54
Podres, Johnny, 31, 41, 50

R
Reese, Pee Wee, 19
retirement, 78–79
Reynaud's phenomenon, 41
Robinson, Jackie, 19
rookies, 17, 19, 22, 32, 64
Roseboro, John, 45, 49

S
San Francisco Giants, 28, 43
Sandy Koufax, 73
Santo, Ron, 64
Sherry, Norm, 31
Skowron, Bill, 49
Snider, Duke, 44

T
Texas Rangers, 88
Thomas, Frank, 36
Tomahawks, 11, 58
Tracewski, Dick, 49

U
University of Cincinnati,
        12, 14

V
Van Heusen Outstanding
        Achievement Award, 76

W
Widmark, Anne (first wife),
        80, 82
Wills, Maury, 36, 44
Wilpon, Fred, 89
World Series, 6, 24–25, 30–31,
        50, 53–54, 67
    1965 Most Valuable Player
        Award, 74

Y
Yom Kippur, 67–68

About the Author

Geraldine Giordano is a New York Yankees fan who lives in Hoboken, New Jersey. She has written two other books for the Rosen Publishing Group, Inc.

Photo Credits

Editor

Jill Jarnow

Series Design and Layout

Geri Giordano